Nature meditation; Types and benefits of nature meditations

Victoria Williams

Table of contents

In the event that you're a nature darling or an ecological lobbyist, you can re-energize your batteries by rehearsing nature contemplation.

To find other reflection rehearses that match your necessities and interests

During nature reflection, you center around at least one of the accompanying: the sights, sounds, scents, or even the taste or feel of nature. In spite of the fact that nature contemplation is normally performed outside, there are likewise nature-themed directed perceptions you can do inside.

Types of nature meditation

What's genuinely going on with meditation

Meditation is a method utilized for millennia to foster familiarity with the current second.

It can include practices to hone concentration and consideration, interface with the body and breath, foster acknowledgment of troublesome feelings, and even modify cognizance.

It's been displayed to offer various physical and mental advantages like pressure reduction and further developed insusceptibility.

While numerous otherworldly customs incorporate contemplation as a piece of their lessons and practices, the actual procedure has a place with no specific religion or confidence.

However old in beginning, it's actually polished today in societies all around the world to make a feeling of harmony, quiet, and inward concordance.

Reflection might offer an answer for the developing need to lessen pressure amidst occupied plans and requesting lives.

Despite the fact that there is definitely not a correct method for thinking, finding a training that addresses your issues is significant.

There are nine famous types of nature meditation

Care meditation

Otherworldly meditation

Centered meditation

Development meditation

Mantra meditation

Supernatural meditation

Moderate unwinding meditation

Cherishing generosity meditation

Representative meditation

Not all meditation styles are appropriate for everybody.

These practices require various abilities and mentalities. How do you have any idea which practice is appropriate for you?

"It feels good and you feel urged to rehearse.

Continue to peruse to get more familiar with the various kinds of contemplation and how to get everything rolling.

1. Care meditation

Care meditation begins from Buddhist lessons and is the most famous and explored type of contemplation in the West.

In care reflection, you focus on your viewpoints as they cross your thoughts. You don't pass judgment on the contemplations or become associated with them. You basically notice and observe any examples.

This training joins focus with mindfulness. You might find it supportive to zero in on an article or your breath while you notice any real sensations, considerations, or sentiments.

This kind of meditation is great for individuals who don't have an instructor to direct them, as it very well may be handily polished alone

2. Otherworldly meditation

Otherworldly meditation is utilized in virtually all religions and profound customs.

The kinds of otherworldly reflection are pretty much as different as the world's profound practices themselves. Large numbers of the contemplation strategies recorded in this article could be viewed as otherworldly reflection.

Otherworldly meditation centers around fostering a more profound comprehension of profound/strict importance and association with a higher power. Models include:

Christian pondering supplication

Recognition of God

Jewish kabbalistic practices

Otherworldly meditation can be drilled at home or in a position of love.

This training is helpful for the individuals who look for profound development and a more profound association with a higher power or otherworldly power.

3. Centered meditation

Centered meditation includes fixation utilizing any of the five senses.

For instance, you can zero in on something inward, similar to your breath, or you can acquire outer impacts to assist with concentrating.

This training might be basic in principle, however it very well may be hard for fledglings to hold their concentration for longer than a couple of moments from the get go.

Assuming your psyche meanders, basically return to the training and pull together.

As the name recommends, this training is great for any individual who needs to hone their concentration and consideration.

4. Development meditation

Albeit a great many people consider yoga when they hear development reflection, this training might include:

strolling
cultivating
qi gong
yoga

Other delicate types of development

This is a functioning type of contemplation where the development guides you into a more profound association with your body and the current second.

Development meditation is really great for individuals who discover an authentic sense of harmony in real life and need to foster body mindfulness.

5. Mantra meditation

Mantra meditation is conspicuous in numerous lessons, including Hindu and Buddhist customs.

This sort of reflection utilizes a redundant sound to clear the brain. It very well may be a word, expression, or sound, one of the most widely recognized being "om."

Your mantra can be spoken uproariously or unobtrusively.

Subsequent to reciting the mantra for quite a while, you'll be more ready and in line with your current circumstance.

This permits you to encounter further degrees of mindfulness.

Certain individuals appreciate mantra contemplation since they find it simpler to zero in on a word than on their breath. Others appreciate feeling the vibration of the sound in their body.

This is likewise a decent practice for individuals who could do without quiet and appreciate reiteration.

6. Supernatural meditation

Supernatural Reflection is a sort of contemplation that has been the subject of various examinations in mainstream researchers.

This training is for the individuals who need an open way to deal with the profundity that contemplation offers.

7. Moderate meditation

Otherwise called body check contemplation, moderate unwinding is a training pointed toward diminishing pressure in the body and advancing unwinding.

Periodically, this type of contemplation includes gradually fixing and loosening up each muscle bunch in turn all through the body.

At times, it might likewise urge you to envision a delicate wave moving through your body to assist with delivering any pressure.

This type of reflection is frequently used to assuage pressure and loosen up before sleep time.

8. Cherishing benevolence meditation

Cherishing benevolence reflection is utilized to reinforce sensations of empathy, generosity, and acknowledgment toward oneself as well as other people.

It ordinarily includes opening the psyche to get love from others and afterward sending kind words to friends and family, companions, associates, and every living being.

Since this sort of reflection is expected to advance sympathy and generosity, it very well might be great for those holding sensations of outrage or hatred.

9. Representation meditation

Representation meditation is a procedure centered around improving sensations of unwinding, harmony, and serenity by picturing positive scenes, pictures, or figures.

This training includes envisioning a scene clearly and utilizing each of the five faculties to add however much detail as could reasonably be expected.

It can likewise include holding a cherished or regarded figure as a top priority determined to exemplify their characteristics.

One more type of perception reflection includes envisioning yourself prevailing at explicit objectives, which is planned to expand concentration and inspiration.

Many individuals use perception reflection to support their temperament, lessen feelings of anxiety, and advance inward harmony

Benefits of nature meditation

It has been irrefutable that the ordinary act of care and contemplation is exceptionally valuable for our psychological,

physical and profound wellbeing. Yet, bringing your training into the regular world external adds another aspect that an indoor reflection setting essentially can't give.

Nature, apparently, has an approach to ordering our consideration and concentration, convincing us to work on our viewpoints and spotlight on common decency before us.

The impacts of pondering in nature can be however enormous as they may be prompt.

Without the steady interruptions that accompany indoor life - and in our computerized world this would incorporate televisions, PCs and cell phones - we become more present, we gain an uplifted feeling of mindfulness.

Additionally, as we take in the regular habitat, we begin to see the straightforward things around us: the breeze, the light, space, sounds and scents.

The following are four different ways that thinking outside can reestablish your body, psyche and soul to a more adjusted condition of wellbeing.

Reinforcing of the brain body association

While being in nature imparts a feeling of careful mindfulness, these faculties are improved when our body and mind can unwind.

Whether we stay situated yet or move our appendages, maybe through moving or strolling, we become more mindful of our actual presence, stance, and equilibrium.

Some reflection techniques intend to rise above the body to advance a condition of loosened up mindfulness.

Facilitating pressure and sorrow

Care has since a long time ago been viewed as a successful method for diminishing side effects of sorrow.

Through the act of reflection, the devices expected to move away from extraordinary gloomy feelings are learned, so those sentiments can be recognized and acknowledged, making it simpler to control them.

This then, at that point, empowers better adapting and the executives of sadness.

Late exploration, including this enormous scope study, have shown that open air reflection rehearses and careful gathering strolls in nature can prompt altogether lower paces of gloom, less pressure and better mental prosperity all round.

Here is a short sky-looking contemplation with care educator and wild aide Imprint Coleman where the wide far reaching perspective on the slope goes about as the magnificent setting

Bringing down circulatory strain

Involving nature and open air space in reflection practice has been demonstrated to yield significant medical advantages.

Notwithstanding the improved feeling of energy and better temperament, the significant actual effects on bringing down circulatory strain and expanding cardiovascular wellbeing ought to be considered carefully.

There are different activities that have reflective advantages like yoga, jujitsu and qigong, and the consolidated effect of development and contemplation advances are still more prominent.

A new report on backwoods washing, an old Japanese practice otherwise called shinrin-yoku, found that actual work in green conditions diminished circulatory strain and stress-related chemicals like cortisol and adrenaline.

The following is an illustration of a maze, an old image that connects with completeness. The symbolism of the circle and the winding are consolidated into an intentional way that is utilized for strolling contemplations.

Further developing fixation

While the steady excitement from our day to day stressors endanger our capacity to keep up with lucidity and concentration, contemplating in nature is the ideal antitoxin that permits us to recharge.

A profoundly helpful encounter emphatically influences our psychological lucidity, as affirmed by ongoing examination that found superior mental capability of the people who invested energy in nature contrasted and the individuals who played out a similar movement in a metropolitan climate.

At the point when you sit on the ground during nature reflections, the body's mood is as one with the world's regular vibrations.

Joined with the absence of surrounding occupied ness, your hearing feels more honed, your skin receptors feel more touchy and your feeling of smell is upgraded.

Why not make an outside care contemplation practice at home a customary piece of your day or week

www.ingramcontent.com/pod-product-compliance
Lightning Source LLC
Chambersburg PA
CBHW060931130726
48001CB00006B/2515